Ripley's Believe It or Not!® Kids

WHAT'S INSIDE?

Take a look at some of the things you'll find inside this crazy book!

PAGE 76

PAGE 74

Loopy lists!
Huge number of hot dogs and other foods eaten very fast!

It's packed, I tell you!

PAGE 112

Wedding Wonders
Meet Princess Fiona and Shrek!

PAGE 27

CHECK THIS OUT!

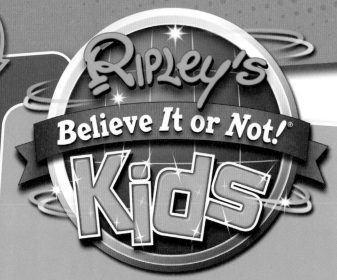

CONTENTS:

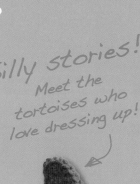

Silly stories! Meet the tortoises who love dressing up!

PAGE 52

TEAR JERKERS

Sea turtles drink salty seawater all their lives. They don't need all of its salt so they cry some of it out in their very **salty tears.**

Seawater has so much salt in it that if you drink it, it would just make you very thirsty!

Crocodiles lose salt through their tongues.

Seagulls drink seawater – they get rid of the unwanted salt in water that **trickles out** through their nose.

Aitchoo!

1 This yellow-spotted river turtle in the Amazon rainforest is surrounded by butterflies that have come to drink its tears.

Turtles have been around for 215 million years!

Keep still.

Gerroff!

2 It is very difficult to find salt in the rainforest, so the butterflies flutter around the turtles' heads to drink their salty tears.

3 If no turtles are around, the butterflies will get their salt from animal wee or sweaty humans!

Bees also drink turtle tears!

THINGS THAT FELL FROM THE SKY

WOAH!

FISH

MEAT

MAGGOTS

Weeeee!

A mass of 2.5 cm long maggots came down in a heavy storm in Acapulco, Mexico, on 5 October, 1968.

Lumps of meat fell from a clear blue sky in Olympian Springs, Kentucky, U.S.A., on 3 March, 1876.

Hundreds of small white fish fell from the sky over the desert town of Lajamanu, Australia, in February 2010.

A shower of peaches fell from the sky onto a building site in Shreveport, Louisiana, U.S.A., on 12 July, 1961.

PEACHES

HEADS

Hundreds of golf balls fell over Punta Gorda, Florida, U.S.A., on 3 September, 1969.

GOLF BALLS

Spiders fell from the sky in Salta Province, Argentina, on 6 April, 2007.

SPIDERS

9

THINGS YOU CAN'T DO IN SPACE

CRY
The tears just stick to your face!

BURP
Weightlessness in space turns any burps into vomit.

THINGS YOU SHOULDN'T TAKE INTO SPACE

SALT AND PEPPER
They would float and could get stuck in an astronaut's eyes and nose. Liquid salt and pepper are used instead.

FARTS
The bad smell stays in the space capsule for too long as there is nowhere for the gas to escape!

THINGS YOU CAN DO IN SPACE

PLAY STAR WARS
In 2007, a genuine light sabre used in the Star Wars movies travelled into space on board the space shuttle.

VOTE
American astronauts can vote in Earth elections from the space station.

TAKE A BATH

Astronauts clean themselves in a watertight shower that sucks away the dirty water.

TASTE

Astronauts lose their sense of taste and smell in space – so they like extra spicy food.

SLEEP IN A BED

Astronauts zip themselves into sleeping bags attached to the walls of the spacecraft so they don't float around.

A SPARE SET OF CLOTHES

Water on a spaceship is too precious for doing laundry.

A COLD

A sneeze floats around for far too long in a spacecraft and its germs have nowhere to go. This could lead to all of the astronauts getting sick.

STUFFED ANIMALS

They smell really bad after time in space.

BREAD

Crumbs could float away and damage equipment.

CARRY THE OLYMPIC TORCH

Two astronauts once carried the Olympic Torch on a spacewalk.

ORDER PIZZA

Pizza Hut delivered a salami pizza in a rocket to a Russian astronaut on the space station.

DRINK YOUR WEE

The space station recycles astronaut urine into water they can drink.

Out of this World Word Search!

Think you're ready to go to space? These word searches will remind you what you can and can't carry or do while you're up there – but you'll need to check the previous pages to figure out what goes where!

TAKE IT INTO SPACE...

```
C M H H Z Z I P E T O V O D W
Y E N C G P X N R O H X O S O
K V M R N H P G H Z G J G I D
L R Q O M H E S Q G N K W J Y
A P S T J Z X E D H Q N O J X
W S T C K V K Z W E L X N C O
E O M I O S O E D B I Z Z Y C
C N B P I Z Z R R M G R I M D
A Z T M I E R F W L H T E H H
P D T Y P T Y P P V T T E C H
S V R L O O U I M W S I V R A
S L H O U N S Z O P A I Y O G
H Y J T Y S R Z E A B P U T W
F S W S W S C A A K R N N V I
A S G A G J H I T A E F C Z V
```

- [ ] Bathe
- [ ] Bread
- [ ] BED
- [ ] Burp
- [ ] Cry
- [ ] Lightsabre
- [ ] Mouthwash
- [ ] Olympic Torch
- [ ] WEE
- [ ] Pepper
- [ ] Pizza
- [ ] Salt
- [ ] Spacewalk
- [ ] Taste
- [ ] Vote

LEAVE IT AT HOME...

```
S B R M J R X U X T P K Z E D
K H G H M C M J R E U B C N P
C F J X Q Z B H E L T A K G Z
C X G J K I G J P G C S Y F C
Z L G V C C U W P I K B A C H
E H T A B N A U E T D W U T Z
R H S T E J Y Y P Y B P X R S
B J Y A W Y D M D P X B U U P
Q R L T W G A Q W E W I H I F
C Z L L Y H Z J J J X L X T H C
S A P M S M T S M N H Q E R D
S W P T E U M U B S D L E V I
N H L D A E R B O O V T T U U
R O V J N O P B V M U N T O S
Q K Z J Y H T E F T V S D E B
```

LITTLE ZOOKEEPER

Charlie Parker the wildlife ranger is only four years old! He has grown up at the Ballarat Wildlife Park in Victoria, Australia, with snakes, frogs and alligators.

SLIMY

Playing with frogs!

Question time...

Q What is your favourite animal?

A The Philippines crocodile. [This is a very rare croc we met at Melbourne Zoo — Charlie's mum].

Q Are there any animals you are afraid of?

A The Taipan snake — it's very poisonous!

Q What is the biggest animal you've ever held?

A Baby, the Burmese python.

Q What do you like best about animals?

A I like all their different colours.

HEAVY

Charlie with Baby, a four-metre-long Burmese python.

TOOTHY

Holding Gump, the baby alligator.

EXTREME WEATHER

Tornado winds can spin at 300 mph and travel at 70 mph.

The wettest place in the world is a village in India called Mawsynram, which gets 12 metres of rainfall every year!

You can't make snowballs at the South Pole – the snow is too dry!

In 1934, a gust of wind on Mount Washington, New Hampshire, U.S.A., was measured at 231 mph.

A hailstone measuring 18 centimetres in diameter – almost as big as a bowling ball – fell in Nebraska, U.S.A., in June 2003.

When you see a bolt of lightning it's actually travelling from the ground upwards, not from the sky downwards.

East Antarctica is the coldest place on Earth. In 2010, the temperature dropped to -57.6°C.

The driest place in the world is the Atacama Desert in Chile. In 1971, rain fell for the first time in 400 years.

Around 6,000 bolts of lightning strike the Earth each minute!

In 1877, a New York newspaper reported that alligators fell from the sky in South Carolina, U.S.A!

A slug's BOTTOM is behind its head.

Pardon?

There are 23 hours, 56 minutes and 4 seconds in a day, not 24 hours.

How high can a penguin jump out of water?

About two metres!

The smallest muscle in your body is in your ear.

A man escaped a python's grip by biting its tail!

Chewing gum is illegal in Singapore.

Snakes never stop growing.

Unlike people, who shrink when they get older!

Animals that lay eggs don't have **belly buttons.**

This includes fish, crocodiles, turtles and birds.

When you blush, the lining of your stomach turns **RED.**

BALLOON MAN

TEENAGE MUTANT NINJA TURTLE

Jeff Wright from Cleveland, Ohio, U.S.A., takes balloon twisting to a whole new level. He transforms himself into famous characters and superheroes, using up to 500 balloons for each amazing costume.

BUZZ LIGHTYEAR

To infinity and beyond!

MARIO

22

Question time...

Q How long have you worked with balloons?

A I started twisting balloons at college, in 2006. I found out quickly that it was a great way to make people smile and make some money. Two years later I made my first costume.

Q How long does it take to make one costume?

A If things go well, I can make a full body costume in 8 hours. If I have to experiment with some tricky designs, it can stretch over a few days. My favourite piece, Buzz Lightyear, took me 10 hours.

Q How do you get in and out of the costumes?

A My costumes are made out of several pieces with my body acting as the skeleton to hold them all together. It's not *too* difficult to get in and out of the costumes, but it's always a good idea to go to the bathroom before putting them on!

IRON MAN

I'm bursting with grrr!

MINIONS!

MONSTER

23

SPOT THE DIFFERENCE!

These pictures may look the same but there are four differences hidden in each of the bottom images! Can you find them all?

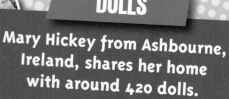

DOLLS

Mary Hickey from Ashbourne, Ireland, shares her home with around 420 dolls.

MORE, MORE, MORE!

SMURFS

In 2009, 2,510 people gathered in Swansea, U.K., dressed as Smurfs, to break the world record.

25

FAMOUS FACES!

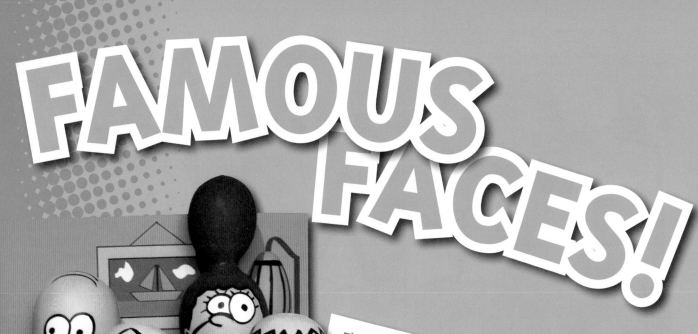

The Simpsons have been painted on eggs by American artist John Lamouranne. He used eggs for their heads, bodies and even for Marge's hair.

The sounds made by Chewbacca in the Star Wars movies were actually moaning camels.

Homer Simpson's catchphrase 'D'oh!' is so famous that it's in the dictionary.

A hot air balloon made in the shape of Darth Vader's mask was launched into the skies over Belgium — it was 26 metres high and 21 metres wide.

Every Doctor Who ever — all eleven of them — have been knitted by Allison Hoffman, from Austin, Texas. She made the dolls for her husband, a huge Doctor Who fan, and each one took five days.

There is a real asteroid between the planets Mars and Jupiter named TARDIS, after Doctor Who's time machine.

POLICE PUBLIC CALL BOX

Shrek-mad fans Amanda Billington and Nathan Gibbs got married dressed as Princess Fiona and Shrek in England in 2013. Everybody else at the wedding had to dress up as well.

Errr...

I hope this green paint washes off Nathan?

The main voice actors in Shrek never actually met each other during the making of the movie.

Dinosaurs had no **eyelashes.**

Tasty!

Squid taste with their tentacles.

There is a town in North Carolina, U.S.A., called chuckle! 'Boogertown'.

MEGA FLUFFBALL!

Just a few more minutes Lucille!

Lucille the English Angora rabbit gets her long fur blow-dried by owner Charlie Lacey before a pet show in California, U.S.A.

ZZZZ...

IS THAT A FACT?

TRUE - ☐
FALSE - ☐

Let's see if you've been paying attention so far. Try to spot which facts are true and which are false.

1. A giant hot air balloon in the shape of Jar Jar Binks flew over Belgium. ☐ ☐

2. Hundreds of **FISH** fell from the sky over the desert town of Lajamanu, Australia, in 2010. ☐ ☐

3. **STUFFED ANIMALS** start to smell bad when you take them into space. ☐ ☐

4. Jeff Wright knits silly costumes out of wool. ☐ ☐

5.  In the rainforest, butterflies drink turtles' TEARS for their salty content. ☐ ☐

6. Dinosaurs had long eyelashes. ☐ ☐

7. Snakes never stop growing. ☐ ☐

8. LIGHTNING travels from the ground up. ☐ ☐

9. When you blush your stomach turns blue. ☐ ☐

10. In 1971, the driest place on Earth – the Atacama Desert – recorded rainfall for the first time in 150 years. ☐ ☐

11. There are exactly 24 hours in a day. ☐ ☐

12. You can't make snowballs at the South Pole. ☐ ☐

31

THE WORLD
Every minute of every day

6,000 lightning strikes

The Sun produces enough energy to power the world for 45 million years

256 BABIES ARE BORN

4,200 flaps of a hummingbird's wings

The International Space Station travels 287 miles

12,000 aeroplanes are in the sky

iPhones are sold **26**

2 MILLION GOOGLE SEARCHES

IN 60 SECONDS
all of these things happen!

100 PEOPLE GET MARRIED

A blue whale's heart beats 10 times

4,500 McDonald's burgers eaten

5 EARTHQUAKES

280,000 stars are born

YOU BLINK ABOUT 20 TIMES (UNLESS YOU ARE ASLEEP)

124 cars are built

1 BILLION ANTS ARE BORN

YOUR HEART BEATS UP TO 110 TIMES

PEEK-A-BOO!

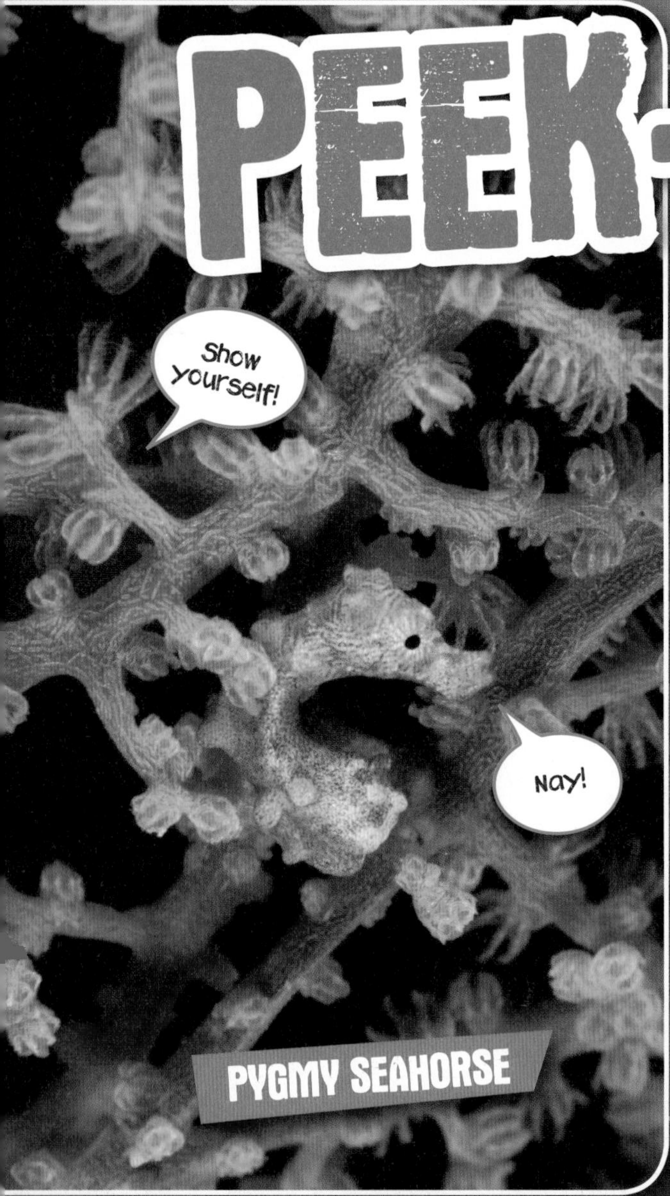
Show yourself!
Nay!
PYGMY SEAHORSE

MOTH

LEAF-TAILED GECKO
Love you Mildred.
I'm over here Norman!

MISSING PUGS!

Wow! There are so many animals it's hard to keep track of them all! Can you find:

A very sleepy cat! ☐

Cats sleep 77% of their lives.

5 hiding pugs!

☐ ☐ ☐ ☐ ☐

A group of pugs is called a grumble!

A smiling crocodile! ☐

Crocs eat rocks! A belly full of rocks helps crocs too digest food and stay underwater.

White peacock

White peacocks have no colours in their feathers, so when the males show off their fine tail feathers, they look like lovely lace fans.

CRAZY COLOURS

Moor frog

Bright pink dragon millipedes are found in Southeast Asia. Their colour warns predators of the poison in their body.

Dragon millipede

Male Moor frogs turn bright blue when they are trying to find a mate. They do this so they can tell the difference between male and female frogs.

Mwanza flat-headed rock agama

Male lizards in this African species have crazy colouring that makes them look just like Spider-Man!

White Bengal tiger

White Bengal tigers are incredibly rare. They don't have the red and yellow pigments (natural colours) in their body that produce a tiger's usual orange fur.

Bright pink slug

Giant pink slugs come out to feed at night on Mount Kaputar in New South Wales, Australia. They grow up to 20 centimetres long!

GLOW FOR IT!

SCARY SCORPION

As if they weren't frightening enough, scorpions can glow in the dark! Their glow may help them to hunt in the darkness.

WEIRD RODENT

This little mouse has been bred to have glow-in-the-dark ears, feet, nose and tail.

FLUORESCENT FUNGUS

Many types of mushrooms glow in the dark, but nobody really knows why!

40

BRIGHT EYE-DEER

Reindeer in Finland have their antlers sprayed with glowing paint to help people spot them in the dark!

GLOWING CAT

Scientists in South Korea have been able to make some cats glow in the dark.

OPEN WIDE

This glowing moray eel was photographed off the coast of the Philippines. They give a nasty bite and have been known to bite diver's fingers off!

OPTICAL ILLUSIONS

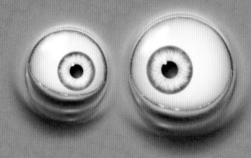

Believe it or not, your brain can be fooled by your own eyes! Check out these optical illusions!

The Blivet is an impossible object! Does it have two legs or three?

You'd get pretty tired climbing the Penrose Stairs as they seem to go up (or down) forever! Yikes!

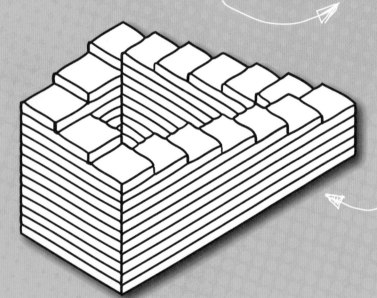

The Penrose Triangle is another impossible object. If you look closely you'll see the sides seem to be twisting in impossible directions!

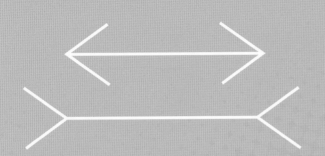

Which arrow is longer? Clue: It's not the one at the bottom! (It's not the one at the top either – in fact, both arrows are the same length! This is called the Müller-Lyer Illusion.)

Believe it or not, the blue circles in the centre of this Ebbinghaus Illusion are exactly the same size!

The Fraser Spiral tricks the eyes – but if you trace one of the lines you'll discover it's not a spiral at all!

In this Bezold Effect, the colour orange looks to be a lighter shade when placed over the white background compared to the black, but in fact, it's exactly the same.

SAY HELLO

Bottle-opener

Old sink

Castle tower

Sniff... I've got a runny nose!

Hey, blockhead!

Watch it!

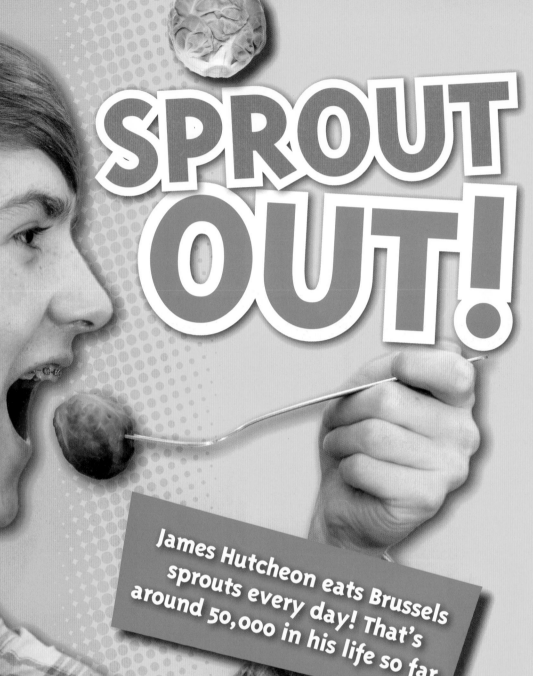

SPROUT OUT!

James Hutcheon eats Brussels sprouts every day! That's around 50,000 in his life so far.

How many types of Brussels sprouts are there?
21

An amazing 38,813 sprouts have been squashed into this Mini! Lawrence Jones spent a day filling the car with them.

What did the world's heaviest sprout weigh?

8 kilograms!

The sprouts in the car weighed the same as 29 reindeer! If laid out end to end, they would be a mile long.

How many Brussels sprouts could you eat in one minute?

The record is 31!

47

INCR-EDIBLE OR INEDIBLE?

Not everything you see here is good enough to eat! Can you tell the yummy treats from the freaky feats?

A ⚪ Incr-edible ⚪ Inedible

Page 100

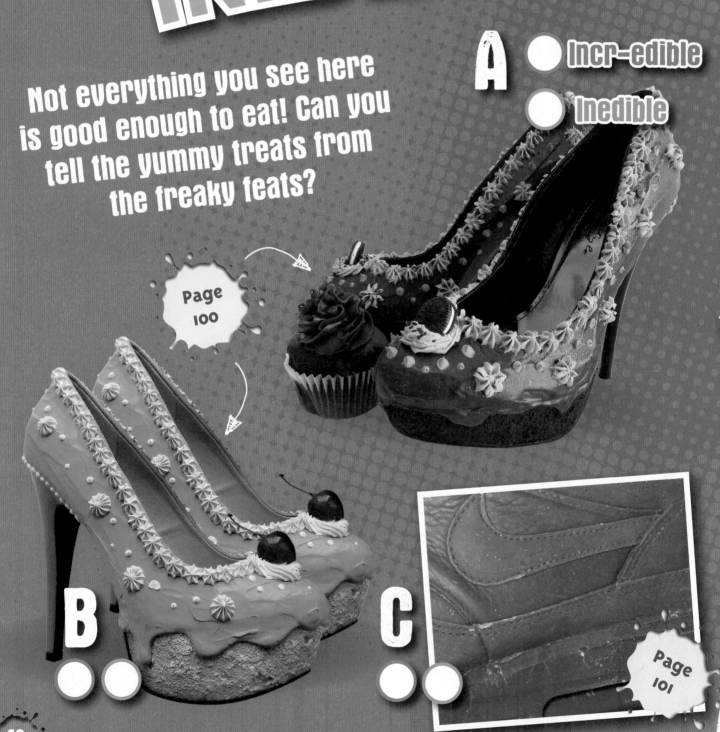

B ⚪ ⚪

C ⚪ ⚪

Page 101

D ● ●

Page 23

E ● ●

Page 50

F ● ●

Page 101

Page 26

Cake International BRONZE

G ● ● ●

H ● ●

I ● ●

Page 95

Page 77

Page 76

J ● ●

K ● ●

L ● ●

If you ate too many carrots, you would turn orange.

I'm so hungry!

The duckbilled platypus has no STOMACH.

More Monopoly money is printed each year than real money!

LONG BODY BITS

Fingernail 1 metre
Melvin Boothe from the U.S.A.

Foot 47 centimetres
Robert Wadlow from the U.S.A.

Hands 31 centimetres
Leonid Stadnyk from Ukraine

Big toe 12.7 centimetres
Matthew McGrory from the U.S.A.

Nose 8.7 centimetres
Mehmet Ozyurek from Turkey

Eyelash 7 centimetres
Stuart Muller from the U.S.A.

Nick Stoeberl from Monterey, California, U.S.A., has a tongue that has been measured at an incredible

10.12 centimetres!

That's big enough to hold FIVE ring doughnuts!

ACTUAL SIZE!

51

Tortoises in Disguise

Tortoise lover Katie Bradley makes stylish clothing for these slow moving animals. The knitted designs, including a birthday cake and a hamburger, make the tortoises easier to see when they are walking across a lawn!

THE REINDEER

THE CHEESEBURGER

Oh, very funny!

THE CRAB

THE SHARK

THE BIRTHDAY CAKE

Hey Bob, your back's on fire!

53

DETECTIVE DOLITTLE NEEDS YOUR HELP...

MUDDLED UP!

These creature names have become muddled up. Can you help Detective Dolittle figure out what they are?

1. Hold Pin

....

2. Has Her Walk

....

3. Pine Gun

....

4. Rock Coach

....

5. Ties Root

....

Guess Who?

These animals are pretty sneaky. Can you recognise them from just a glimpse?

A

B

C

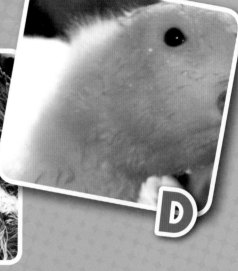

D

Migration Patterns

Can you find the following animals hidden in the grid?

☐ Snail
☐ Bear
☐ Dog
☐ Cat
☐ Rat

```
U K E X F Y X T R B H S
Z T R S E I E Y T D C Q
P E A C O C K Y A X V M
D V A L K N S L C H T O
H B X G R M T I F E M N
I E C I A L T A R W I K
E A Q Q H N N N G V T E
F R I X S R A S H W V Y
P Y T H O N E A E M N E
A Q T F V J Z G O D X I
W G Q Z S K B G U Q Y T
B L U G S Z Y A Q T K D
```

☐ Shark
☐ Monkey
☐ Tiger
☐ Peacock
☐ Python

GANGNAM BEAR!

This wild brown bear cub was spotted showing off in front of his mum doing his best Gangnam Style dance!

Cockroaches have extra teeth in their **stomach.**

Wearing pyjamas in public is popular in Shanghai, China. They have 'pyjama police' to try to stop people doing it!

It wasn't me officer!

Humans shed **four kilograms** of skin each year!

57

YOUR BODY IN NUMBERS

You have roughly **100 BILLION** brain cells, called neurons.

You have around **3 TRILLION** pores (tiny holes) in your skin.

We lose around **100** hairs a day.

An adult makes around **3.5 pints of spit a day.** That's roughly 160 gallons a year!

There are **650** muscles in the human body. Your biggest muscle is in your backside.

You fart **14** times a day on average. This is likely to go up if you eat a lot of beans!

Average number of breaths taken by a human each day = **23,000**

Average number of heartbeats a day = **100,000** That's 35 million a year.

THERE ARE 5 MILLION

hairs on the adult human body, on average (some people are hairier than others).

The small and large intestine are around **7.92 metres** long in total in an adult. They are curled up in the stomach.

DRIVING DIFFERENCES!

These pictures don't look real – but they are! However, if you look closely you'll find there are four differences hidden in each. Try to find them all!

Move those candles, I can't see where I'm going!

This motorised dining table travels at an incredible 113 mph! It was created by Perry Watkins, from England, who can be seen driving from beneath the turkey in the middle of the 'car'.

GAS

Old gas station in Zillah, Washington, U.S.A.

Milk and Sugar sir?

Fill 'er up please.

This two-seater toilet car, built by Dave Hersch from Lakewood, Colorado, U.S.A., can hit speeds of 30 mph! Dave and his ten-year-old son, Miles, ride it around their local neighbourhood.

SLOSH!

61

WOOF WEDDING

Lucky pups Lanlan and Guaiguai got married at an animal rescue centre in China. They each wore a special wedding outfit and were given a marriage certificate.

There are

3 CHICKENS

for every person on Earth.

PING!

An electric eel can produce enough power to run a

microwave.

One day on Venus lasts for 117 Earth days.

WHEELY COOL!

Septimus the tortoise is back on the move after having his front legs replaced with model aeroplane wheels. The 23-year-old pet had the surgery after being injured. He is now able to turn himself around and go backwards, which he couldn't do before.

A praying mantis has just one ear, and it's on its stomach!

whooosh!

AMAZING

Chicky the dolphin has learned how to paint! She holds a paintbrush in her mouth, and carefully paints colourful brush strokes on a canvas next to her pool.

A hippopotamus can run faster than a man.

SNAIL'S PACE

Hurry up!

This dozing frog couldn't be bothered to move when a slimy snail decided to slide over it. Being a snail, it took eight minutes to complete the move!

ANIMALS!

At birth, a baby kangaroo is smaller than a cherry.

COLD FEET?

This striking seabird is a blue-footed booby, named for (you guessed it!) its bright blue feet. The brighter the better, as females pick the males with the bluest feet to be their mate.

PUZZLE IT OUT!

Animal Puzzle

Fill in the animals from Charlie Parker's zoo and discover the hidden word down the centre.

Animals to add:

- Bee
- Frog
- Snake
- Python
- Lizards
- Reptiles
- Alligator

Read more about Charlie and his zoo on pages 14–15.

The hidden word is:

. . . .

RIPLEY'S CROSSWORD

Across:

5. Pogonophobia is the fear of these (6)
9. Ants are able to lift items many times their weight because they are this (6)
10. This long-necked animal can survive without water even longer than a camel (7)
12. Charlie Parker is a little ...... keeper (3)
13. Ripley's .... it or ...... (7, 3)
15. In the rainforest, butterflies try to drink this animal's salty tears (6)
16. Feline which can be either left or right handed (3)

Down:

1. Something you can't do in space – because it makes you vomit! (4)
2. These aquatic creatures fell from the sky over Lajamanu, Australia, in 2010 (4)
3. The males of this type of frog are coloured blue (4)
4. No matter where they are in the world, every single one of these black and white bears belongs to China (6)
6. Tornados are one example of this kind of weather (7)
7. This strikes the Earth 6,000 times a minute (9)
8. Lawrence Jones filled a Mini car with Brussels .... (7)
10. All scorpions do this in the dark (4)
11. To drink like a duck (6)
14. The smallest muscle in your body is located here (and it helps you to hear!) (3)
15. Name of the adventurous spaniel who loves to snowboard, surf and fly (4)

Most frogs don't drink WATER.

Snowflakes can take as long as **one hour** to fall to the ground.

We are about 2.5 cm **TALLER** in the morning than we are in the evening. Fluid in our joints builds up each night and adds to our height, but is squashed down during the day.

TOYBOY

Bess the cow-horned boxfish fell in love with a spiky plastic toy that was popped into her tank in Great Yarmouth. She thought her cute toy-boyfriend was a boxfish, too.

Say you feel the same way about me.

One of a cockroach's favourite foods is the glue on the back of stamps.

Delicious!

So tasty!

NAMELESS is the name of a town in Texas.

Forget stamp glue, you should try web!

Spiders recycle their webs by eating them!

A giraffe can go **without water** longer than a camel can.

Until 1911, clocks in French railway stations were set five minutes fast **so people wouldn't miss their trains.**

you bet!

Mel Blanc (the voice of Bugs Bunny) didn't like **CARROTS!**

71

ROAD HOGS GAME!

Believe it or snort, these pigs love to race! And now is your chance to join in. Find a friend, choose a pig and get racing! Chop, chop!

You Will Need:

- 2 – 4 players
- 1 counter each (Cut out from bottom right corner)
- A die

How to Play:

1. Each player chooses a pig and places it on the starting line.

2. Roll to see who starts — highest goes first (roll again if two people get the same!).

3. Each player makes their way around the track, following the instructions on each square.

4. Believe it or not, the winner is the one whose pig reaches the finish line first!

72

Shown a short cut by a super smart dog-trot onto...

Monkey on your back! Roll a 4, 5 or 6 to move!

Page 107

Slowed down by a slug — miss a go!

Page 18

Shark attack! Roll again, but whatever you get you must go that number of squares backwards!

Slowed down by snails! On your next go, you can only move if you roll a 1 or 2.

Page 92

Jumping penguins block your way! Go back to...

Page 18

Start

1
2
3
4

Slow-moving sloth crossing the track — miss a go!

Page 93

Struck by lightning — zap forward three spaces.

Slide down an elephant's trunk...

Page 74

Page 77

First to the trough, roll again!

Page 95

Hurry back two squares to avoid poisonous millipede.

Blown back five squares by a twister!

Page 38

Shown a short cut by a blue-footed booby, trot forward to...

Page 65

Fly past your opponents! Roll again!

Covered in bees! Throw the die twice, then take the lowest number for your next roll.

Page 19

Slip on a slippery snake. Go back to...

Finish

Scissors are SHARP! Ask an adult for help before using.

73

Elephants suck their trunks like children suck their thumbs.

To have your photo taken with the first camera ever invented, you would have to sit still for eight hours!

Ice in the Antarctic is more than 2.5 miles thick in places.

Dogs and cats, like humans, are either right or left handed.

I still can't tell my right from my left though.

In Ancient Rome, people whitened their teeth using wee!

A bolt of lightning contains enough energy to toast **160,000** pieces of bread.

Unfortunately the bolt only lasts 1/10,000th of a second, so turning the bread over might be hard!

Missed again! Why can't we just get a toaster like everybody else?

AWESOME EATERS!

GULP!

ADRIAN MORGAN ATE

20 BOILED EGGS

IN 84 SECONDS!

JAMIE 'THE BEAR' McDONALD ATE

3 kilograms OF ONION RINGS

IN 8 MINUTES!

SONYA THOMAS ATE

445 OYSTERS

IN 5 MINUTES!

TAKERU KOBAYASHI ATE

110 HOT DOGS

IN 10 MINUTES!

MOLLY SCHUYLER ATE A

72-OZ STEAK

IN 2 MINUTES, 44 SECONDS!

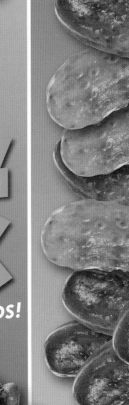

JOE LaRUE ATE

1.8 kilograms of PICKLES

IN 5 MINUTES!

FACT OR FAKE?

Think you know your facts from your fakes? See if you can spot the five fakes among the eight real ones.

TRUE – ☐
FALSE – ☐

GO

1
More Monopoly money is printed each year than real money.
☐ ☐

2
Cockroaches have extra teeth in their stomachs.
☐ ☐

3
All the pandas in the world belong to Japan.
☐ ☐

4
A hippopotamus can run faster than a man.
☐ ☐

5
There are 100 teeth in a great white shark's mouth.
☐ ☐

6
Turnips turn red when sunburnt.
☐ ☐

7
We have the same number of hairs on our bodies as a chimpanzee.
☐ ☐

9
In Ancient Rome, people brushed their teeth with poo!
☐ ☐

8
You can make a battery out of lemons.
☐ ☐

12
There are 20 different types of Brussels sprouts.
☐ ☐

10
A slug's bottom is behind its head.
☐ ☐

11
Your biggest muscle is your backside (or your bottom)!
☐ ☐

13
The blood of a spider is light blue.
☐ ☐

Horseshoe Crabs
have eyes on their tail.

We're pretty mixed up!

AN ADULT SPEAKS ABOUT **16,000** WORDS A DAY.

BIG NOSE
WORLD CHAMPIONSHIPS
have been held every year since 1961 in Langenbruck, Germany!

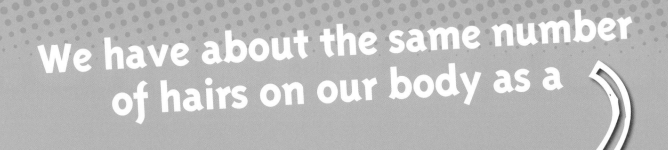

We have about the same number of hairs on our body as a

There are about three million shipwrecks on the ocean floor.

yeh, so think twice before you call me a hairy ape!

Tropical velvet worms catch their insect prey with sticky ropes of slime squirted from their head.

BIG NUMBERS!

93,000,000 miles from the Earth to the Sun

180,497 islands in the world

7257.48 kilograms = weight of shrimp-like creatures (crustaceans) a blue whale eats each day

4 is the only number that has the same number of letters as the number itself

10,000,000,00

100,000,000,000,000 cells in your body

32 muscles in a cat's ear

44 squirts of a cow's udder makes 1 pint of milk

300

teeth in a great white shark's mouth

6,000,000,000
dust mites live in an average bed

20,000,000,000
jellyfish live in Jellyfish Lake, an island in Palau

1,000,000,000
= approximate number of cars in the world

7,000,000,000
= estimated population on Earth

0,000,000,000
insects thought to be alive at any moment

1
OUT OF
EVERY 10
humans are left-handed

21,000,000
= approximate number of footsteps a person would take to walk around the Earth

NUMBER PROBLEMS

THE CODE WORD THAT FELL FROM THE SKY!

Crack the code to uncover what items fell from the sky, you can always check 'The Things That Fell From The Sky' on pages 8-9 if you get stuck!

Grid (by row):

Row 1: 16
Row 2: 5
Row 3: 13, 1, 7, 7, 15, 20, 19, 1
Row 4: 15, 16, 3
Row 5: 12, 6, 9, 19, 8
Row 6: 6, 4, 5
Row 7: 2, 5, 19
Row 8: 13, 5, 1, 20, 18
Row 9: 12, 19
Row 10: 12
Row 11: 19

Code key:

#	Letter	#	Letter
1	A	14	N
2	B	15	O
3	C	16	P
4	D	17	Q
5	E	18	R
6	F	19	S
7	G	20	T
8	H	21	U
9	I	22	V
10	J	23	W
11	K	24	X
12	L	25	Y
13	M	26	Z

MAKE EVERY MOMENT COUNT!

SUDOKU CHALLENGE

It's time to make sure everything adds up! Can you help complete this five by five Sudoku grid, ensuring that every horizontal and vertical line contains the numbers one to five?

			5	1
2	5			
1		4		
				3
5		3	4	

SEE YOU!

Some spiders can walk on water.

Tarantulas deep fried with salt and garlic are a popular snack in Cambodia.

Some spiders are as large as a dinner plate!

Water spiders live underwater.

Some female spiders eat their male mates.

Jumping spiders can jump up to six times their own height.

The blood of a spider is light blue.

YOU LOOKIN'

Match these animal eyes to their owners in the list below. Can you spot the odd one out?

Goat • Crocodile fish • Llama
Macaw • Horse • Elephant
Hornbill • Owl butterfly • Cat
Mossy frog • Lizard

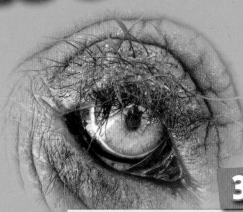

3
....

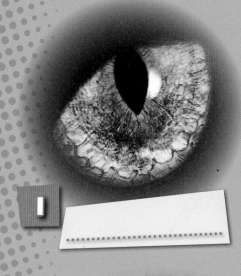

1
....

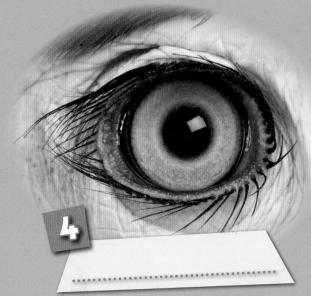

4
....

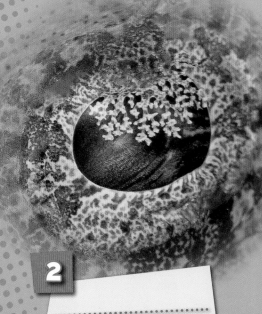

2
....

5
....

AT ME?

7
....

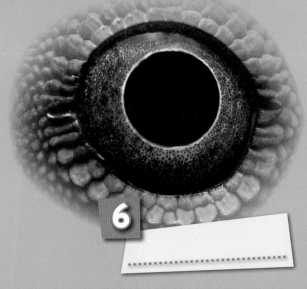

6
....

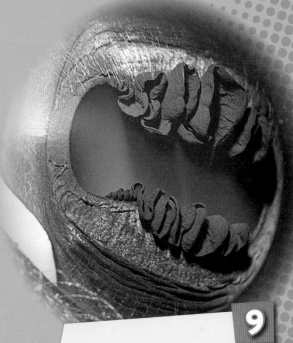

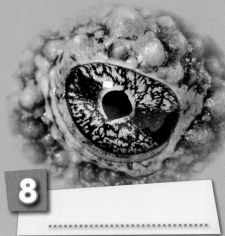

8
....

9
....

11
....

10
....

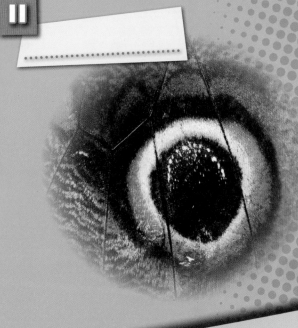

ANIMAL CRACK-UPS!

G'DAY!

These cute wallaby babies look the same but there are six differences in the pictures. Can you find them all?

These adorable little orphan wallabies are being cared for in an animal shelter in New South Wales, Australia. They have their own cosy pouches made from second-hand clothes.

These animals can't be real, can they? However, if you look closely, you should be able to spot which four animals went into making each of them!

A

This animal is made up from:

1 . . . .
2 . . . .
3 . . . .
4 . . . .

B

1 . . . .
2 . . . .
3 . . . .
4 . . . .

C

1 . . . .
2 . . . .
3 . . . .
4 . . . .

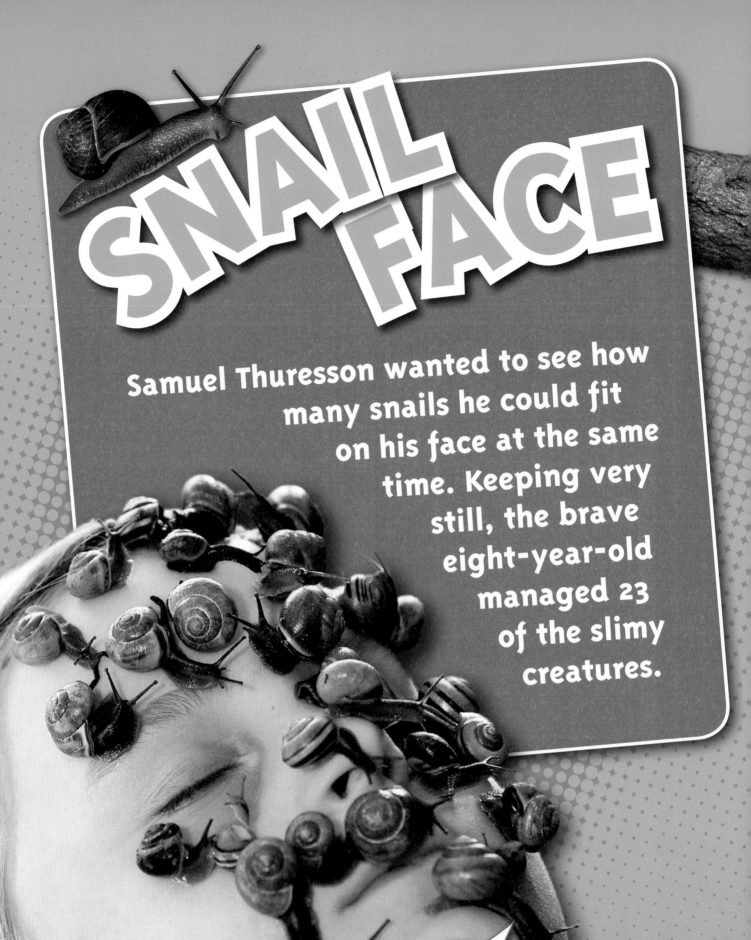

SNAIL FACE

Samuel Thuresson wanted to see how many snails he could fit on his face at the same time. Keeping very still, the brave eight-year-old managed 23 of the slimy creatures.

Come on guys, let's crawl down his shirt!

Sloths move at just 0.15 mph.

...98, 99, 100. coming, ready or not!

Turnips turn GREEN when sunburnt.

Crayfish signal to each other by weeing from a gland on their HEADS!

DOG DAYS

Teka the four-year-old papillon spaniel is a sporting superstar. Her owners took her snowboarding and she loved it so much that they decided to try some other sports. Now she enjoys surfing and even flying under a bunch of balloons. That's one daring dog!

check out these moves!

Surfing

Snowboarding

Flying

woohoo!

Question time...

We asked Teka's owners, Jim and Amanda Holmdahl, all about their amazing dog.

Q How did you teach Teka these sports?

A Teka picks up new sports easily because when people are watching her she will do something over and over again. She loves the attention!

Q When and how did Teka learn to fly?

A She started flying in 2013 — we trained her on a zip line between two tall trees.

Q What is Teka's favourite sport?

A Her favourite sport is chasing our two cats, and her second favourite is flying!

WATER MAGIC

HERE ARE SOME COOL TRICKS TO TRY AT HOME. ALL YOU NEED IS SOME WATER AND A FEW EASY-TO-FIND EXTRAS.

REVERSING DIRECTION

YOU WILL NEED:

- A sheet of paper
- A pen
- A clear glass of water

Draw two or three arrows on a sheet of paper, making sure that all arrows point to the left.

Stand the paper up against a wall. Now place a glass of water in front of the paper so that you can look through it to see the paper. No way!!! The arrows have changed direction! Now they point to the right!

RUNAWAY PEPPER!

YOU WILL NEED:

- A large bowl
- Pepper
- Water
- Washing up liquid

First, fill a bowl with tap water. Then, sprinkle some pepper into the bowl. Sprinkle a lot so that you can see what happens.

The pepper should spread out on the surface of the water.
Now try dipping your finger in — nothing special happens, does it? Put a little coating of washing up liquid on your finger — just a dab is fine — then try putting your finger into the bowl again to see what happens. The pepper runs away — and that's nothing to sneeze at!

DIVE IN!

YOU WILL NEED:

- A see-through plastic bottle
- An unopened packet of ketchup from a fast-food restaurant
- Some water

Place the unopened ketchup packet into the bottle. Top up the bottle with water leaving a centimetre or so at the top (it doesn't need to be completely full), then seal it closed.

The ketchup packet should float somewhere close to the middle of the bottle. Now try squeezing the bottle. When you do, the ketchup packet should sink to the bottom. Stop squeezing and the ketchup will rise back towards the top of the bottle just like a deep sea diver! That's amazing!

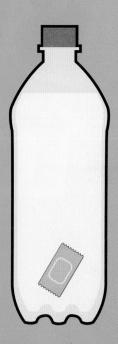

BENDING WATER

YOU WILL NEED:

- A cold water tap — a bathroom or kitchen tap is fine
- A plastic comb (or you could also use a balloon instead)

First, comb your hair vigorously with the comb (or you can also try rubbing your hair with the inflated balloon). Next, turn on the tap so that just a thin stream of water is coming out. Now, place your comb (or balloon) near to the stream of flowing water and watch what happens. The water should bend away from the comb (or balloon). What? Does water get scared?!!

Big mouth!

Whale sharks suck prey into their giant mouth, which is so big that this diver was almost sucked inside. Luckily they only eat tiny creatures — they would spit out a human!

Woah, stop creeping up on me!

They can hang beneath schools of fish and 'vacuum' them up.

One whale shark was followed swimming around the Pacific Ocean — it swam 8,078 miles in 37 months!

The whale shark...

...lives for over 70 years.

...is the world's largest fish, growing to over 12 metres in length.

...has a mouth up to 1.5 metres wide, which contains around 350 rows of tiny teeth.

Each whale shark has a different pattern of spots on its back.

They have the thickest skin of any animal. It is over 10 centimetres thick in some places.

Too good to eat?

Breakfast food painting
by Prudence Staite

Fake cake shoes
by Chris Campbell

Fashion designer Chris Campbell, from Florida, U.S.A., makes footwear that looks like fabulous food. The yummy decorations on his cake-style shoes aren't real, though. You can look at them, and wear them, but you can't lunch on them!

Gummy bear
chandelier
by YaYa Chou

Lion cake
by Steph Parker

Cake
International
BRONZE
won by
No7. STEPHANIE PARKER

Chocolate
trainer
by Joost Goudriaan

Christmas
dinner cake!
by Annabel de Vetten

101

CRAZY DAYS!

The annual U.K. **WORM CHARMING** festival sees competitors trying to tempt worms out of the ground. The record is 567!

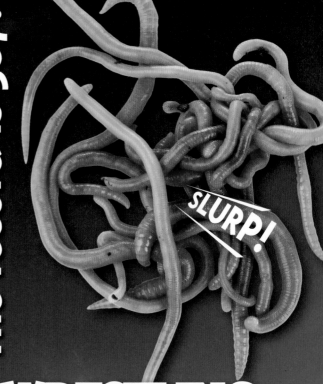

SLURP!

THE WORLD TOE-WRESTLING CHAMPIONSHIPS

takes place in the U.K. in August.

On a special day each November **DOGS ARE WORSHIPPED** in Nepal, at the festival of Kukur Tihar.

At the Norwegian **Ice Music Festival** each February, musicians play instruments made out of ice.

La Tomatina is a giant **TOMATO THROWING** battle held in the Spanish town of Buñol every August.

Each February in Ivrea, Italy, thousands of townspeople get into nine teams to take part in the **Battle of the Oranges.** They throw the fruit at each other for three days!

The Christmas Tree-Throwing World Championships are held each year in Germany.

A village in Spain holds a **GOAT-TOSSING** festival in January, where a goat is thrown out of a church tower and caught, unharmed, by the crowd below.

International Pillow Fight Day takes place each April in cities across the world.

MATCH THE FACTS!

Can you match the right fact to the right question?

1. La Tomatina
2.  567
3. Dogs
4. PILLOWS
5. FROM A CHURCH TOWER
6. Ivrea, Italy
7. ICE
8. TOE
9. CHRISTMAS TREE

If you're not sure, check out the previous page for all the facts!

A A village in Spain drops a goat from this.

B Record number of worms charmed at the Annual U.K. Worm Charming contest.

C Musical instruments are made from this at a special music festival held in Norway.

D The annual Battle of the Oranges takes place here.

E The name of the famous tomato throwing battle held each year in Spain.

F An annual German championship involves throwing this item.

G This type of fight takes place every April in cities across the world.

H Worshipped in the Nepalese festival of Kukur Tihar.

I A wrestling championship held every August in the U.K. involves this.

BEAST BUDDIES

Here's a furry feel-good story. This monkey in Thailand was rescued after a dog attack, and now lives with his gentle rabbit friend, Toby.

Brock the baby otter and Bumble Bee the badger cub became best friends at their wildlife centre in Somerset.

Australian Dalmatian dog Zoe made friends with an orphaned black-and-white lamb. The lamb soon began to think he was a dog and slept in Zoe's kennel.

This baby monkey hitched a ride on a lion cub while playing with some baby tigers at a tiger park in China.

Over at Noah's Ark Farm near Bristol, Gerald the giraffe and Eddie the goat have buddied up. They look out for each other in the Africa enclosure, which they share with a bunch of zebras.

GROSS-OUT Eyeball Cakes!

Creep out your friends and family by giving them one of these super gross eyeball cakes!

You will need:

- 125 g soft margarine
- 125 g caster sugar
- 2 large eggs
- 125 g self raising flour
- 1 tsp vanilla essence
- 1 tub vanilla icing
- Green food colouring
- Some round sweets (liquorice allsorts are ideal!)

Remember: Always ask an adult to help when cooking.

What to do:

1. Mix the margarine and sugar together until light and fluffy, then beat in the eggs one at time along with a tablespoon of flour.

2. Add the vanilla essence and fold in the remaining flour.

3. Line a cake tin with paper cases and half fill each case with the mixture.

4. Bake in an oven preheated to 180°C/350°F/GM-4 for 12 minutes.

5. You can tell that the cakes are done when they have risen up, are golden in colour and spring back into shape when pressed lightly with your finger.

6. Once they are done, remove the cakes and let them cool on a wire rack.

7. Colour half of the icing green (or any colour of your choice) by mixing in some green food colouring, leaving the other half white.

8. Then, ice the cakes with white (for the white of the eyes) and green for the iris.

9. For a finishing touch, decorate them with a round sweet each to create the centre of the eye.

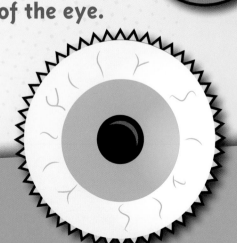

Top tip:
You can try other coloured eyes – like blue and brown. You could even make the eyes bright red! Yikes!

Ant-astic strength!

Tiny weaver ants can hold onto objects, such as these pencils, that are hundreds of times heavier than their own bodies — that's like you carrying a whale!

The tiny moss mite is the strongest creature on Earth! It can hold 1,180 times its own weight, which is like a human lifting up a jumbo jet.

The froghopper bug can leap 100 times its own length!

Tigers can carry prey weighing 500 kg — that's twice their own body weight — up a tree.

An African elephant is strong enough to carry over **100 humans at once** — if they could all fit on its back!

If you were as strong as a rhinoceros beetle you could...

walk a mile with a car on your head!

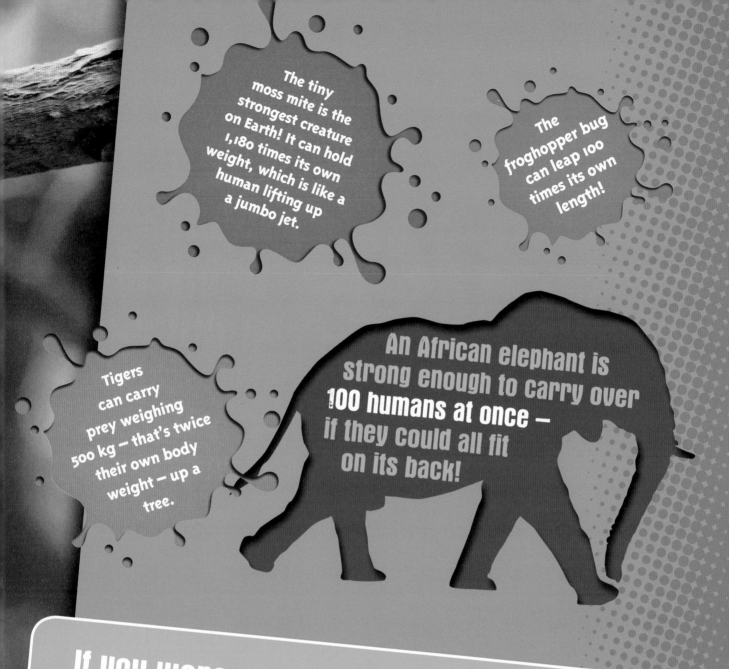

Hmm, more like 'dribble'. I wish I had lips!

DIBBLE means to drink like a duck.

You can make a battery out of lemons.

Queen bumblebees go BALD in old age.

A drop of ocean water takes 1,000 years to travel around the world.

All the pandas in the world belong to CHINA.

Grizzly bears can eat up to 40 kilograms of food a day. That's equivalent to 360 quarter pounder burgers from McDonald's.

BE AFRAID!

A phobia is an extreme fear of something, and every phobia has a name.

POGONOPHOBIA IS THE FEAR OF **BEARDS**

Parthenophobia is the fear of GIRLS

Coulrophobia is the fear of CLOWNS

Clinophobia IS THE FEAR OF GOING TO BED

Scoleciphobia is the fear of **Worms**

Ambulophobia is the fear of WALKING

Anthophobia IS THE FEAR OF **FLOWERS**

Koumpounophobia is the fear of **buttons**

HIPPOPOTOMONSTROSESQUIPPEDALIOPHOBIA is the fear of LONG WORDS

ZOOPHOBIA is the fear of ANIMALS

Tonsurephobia is the fear of haircuts

TUROPHOBIA is the fear of CHEESE

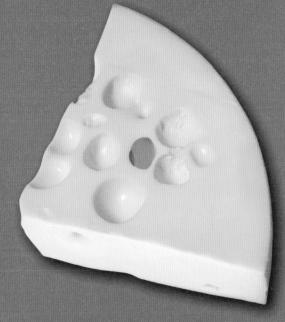

Triskaidekaphobia IS THE FEAR OF THE Number 13

OMBROPHOBIA is the fear of RAIN

AILUROPHOBIA is the fear of CATS

FEAR OF QUIZZES QUIZ

Don't be afraid! Here are twenty fearful phobias and all you have to do is say if they're true or false! Pretty scary stuff, huh?

T F

☐ ☐ 1. Arachnophobia – fear of spiders

☐ ☐ 2. Entomophobia – fear of insects

☐ ☐ 3. Zoophobia – fear of people called 'Zoe'

☐ ☐ 4. Thermophobia – fear of heat

☐ ☐ 5. Ringringringringringringophobia – fear of telephones

☐ ☐ 6. Phonophobia – fear of loud noises

☐ ☐ 7. Hypnophobia – fear of hips

13

- [ ] [ ] 8. Hexakosioihexekontahexaphobia – fear of the number 666
- [ ] [ ] 9. Phasmophobia – fear of ghosts
- [ ] [ ] 10. Chaetophobia – fear of cheats
- [ ] [ ] 11. Emetophobia – fear of time travel
- [ ] [ ] 12. Astraphobia – fear of thunder and lightning
- [ ] [ ] 13. Triskaidekaphobia – fear of the number 13
- [ ] [ ] 14. Chiroptophobia – fear of back injury
- [ ] [ ] 15. Darkophobia – fear of the dark
- [ ] [ ] 16. Hylophobia – fear of greeting people
- [ ] [ ] 17. Omphalophobia – fear of belly buttons
- [ ] [ ] 18. Melissophobia – fear of people called 'Melissa'
- [ ] [ ] 19. Decidophobia – fear of making decisions
- [ ] [ ] 20. Panphobia – fear of saucepans

BANG

LOST IN SPACE

NO WAY!

UNDERPANTS

Astronauts on the International Space Station fire their dirty underwear into space.

CAMERAS

Two cameras were dropped by astronauts on spacewalks, never to be seen again.

Astronaut Alan Shepard hit two golf balls on the surface of the Moon — they travelled for miles!

GOLF BALLS

TOOL BAG

A tool bag was dropped on a spacewalk — it travelled around Earth 4,000 times and was big enough to see with a telescope.

POOP

Astronaut poop is fired out into space and burns up in the Earth's atmosphere.

A spatula floated off into space when an astronaut used it to repair a space shuttle.

PLIERS

A pair of pliers disappeared into space from the space shuttle, Discovery.

RUBBISH

Bags of rubbish are thrown out of the International Space Station, but burn up before reaching Earth!

SPATULA

ASHES

The ashes of Gene Roddenberry, creator of the Star Trek TV series, were fired into space.

GLOVE

An astronaut's glove travelled at 17,500 mph around the Earth for a month before burning up in the atmosphere!

WEE

Astronauts wee is pumped out into space where it freezes.

119

SLOW BOAT

Twenty men from Estonia managed to pull along a giant cruise ship that weighed twenty million kilograms. Some of these mega-muscly men have also successfully pulled jet planes and trains!

Tom Sietas swam **120 metres** underwater in one breath in 2008.

In 2011, James Roumeliotis spent 20 hours bouncing on a pogo stick — that's over **200,000** bounces!

French climber Alain 'Spider-Man' Robert once climbed the 381-metre-high Empire State building — with no ropes.

Hungarian strongman Zsolt Sinka can pull a 50,000 kilogram Airbus aeroplane, over 30 metres — with his teeth!

Yea, I tried it last year and I haven't been able to stand up since!

Benoît Lecomte swam **3,700 miles** across the Atlantic in 73 days.

Answers

Pg 12 – 13

INTO SPACE...

```
C M H I Z Z I P E T O V O D W
Y E N C G P X N R O H X O S O
K V M R N H P G H Z G J G I D
I R Q O M H E S Q G N K W J Y
A P S T J Z X D H Q N O J X
V S T C K V K Z W E L X N C O
E O M I O S O E D B I Z Z Y C
C N B P I Z Z R R M G R I M D
A Z T M I E R F W L I T E H H
P D T Y P T Y P P V T T E C H
I S V R L O O U I M W S L I V R A
S L H O U N S L O P A I Y O G
H Y J T Y S R Z E A S P U T W
F S W S W S C A A K R N N V I
A S G A G J H I T A I F C Z V
```

LEAVE IT AT HOME...

```
S B R M J R X U X T P K Z E D
K H G H M C M J R E U B C N P
C F J X Q Z B H E L T A K G Z
C X G J K I G J P G C S Y F C
Z L G V C C U W P I K B A C H
E H T A D N A U E T D W U T Z
R H S T E J Y Y P Y B P X I S
B J Y A W Y D M D P X B U U P
Q Z L Y G A Q W E W I H I F
C Z L Y H Z J J X L X T H C
S A P M S M T S M N H Q E R D
S W P T E U M U B S D L E V I
N H L D A E R D O O V T T U U
R O V J N O P B V M U N T O S
Q K Z J Y H T E E T H S D E D
```

Pg 24 – 25

Pg 30 – 31

1. FALSE	5. TRUE	9. FALSE
2. TRUE	6. FALSE	10. FALSE
3. TRUE	7. TRUE	11. FALSE
4. FALSE	8. TRUE	12. TRUE

Pg 36 – 37

Pg 48 – 49

A. DON'T EAT	E. DON'T EAT	I. DON'T EAT
B. DON'T EAT	F. EAT	J. DON'T EAT
C. EAT	G. EAT	K. EAT
D. EAT	H. EAT	L. EAT

Pg 54

1. DOLPHIN
2. WHALE SHARK
3. PENGUIN
4. COCKROACH
5. TORTOISE

Pg 55

A. GIRAFFE
B. CHIMPANZEE
C. SPIDER
D. DUCK

```
U K E X F Y X T R B H S
Z T R S E I E Y T D C Q
P E A C O O K Y A X V M
D V A L K N S L C H T O
H B X G R M T I F E M N
I E C I A L T A R W I K
E A Q Q H N N N G V T E
F R I X S R A S H W V Y
P Y T H O N E A E M N E
A Q T F V I Z C O D X I
W G Q Z S K B G R Q Y T
B L U G S Z Y A Q T K D
```

Pg 60 – 61

Pg 66

```
F R O G
L I Z Z A R D
R E P T I L E S
A L L I G A T O R
B E E
P Y T H O N
S N A K E
```

THE HIDDEN WORD IS:
RIPLEYS

122

Pg 67

(crossword)

Across/Down letters:
- MOO
- PANDAS
- BEARDS
- BUS
- FISH
- STRONG
- EXTREA (EXTREA...)
- GIRAFFE
- LIGHTING
- SPROUTS
- GLOW
- ZOO
- BELIEVENOT
- DIBBLE
- EAR
- TURTLE
- TEK
- CAT

Pg 88 – 89

1. CAT
2. CROCODILE FISH
3. ELEPHANT
4. HORNBILL
5. HORSE
6. LIZARD
7. MACAW
8. MOSSY FROG
9. LLAMA
10. GOAT
11. OWL BUTTERFLY—this is the odd one out as it's not the real eye, it's the pattern on its wing!

Pg 90

Pg 91

IMAGE A
1. DUCK - HEAD
2. PYTHON - NECK
3. PENGUIN - BODY
4. FROG - FEET

IMAGE B
1. DEER - ANTLERS
2. GOAT - HEAD
3. BEAR - BODY
4. CAT - FEET

IMAGE C
1. CAMEL - HEAD
2. GIRAFFE - NECK
3. BLUE FOOTED BOOBY (BIRD) - BODY
4. ELEPHANT - FEET

Pg 78 – 79

1. TRUE
2. TRUE
3. FALSE
4. TRUE
5. FALSE
6. FALSE
7. TRUE
8. TRUE
9. FALSE
10. TRUE
11. TRUE
12. FALSE
13. TRUE

Pg 84

(word grid: MAGGOTS, PEACHES, WOLFBALLS, SPIDERS, FISH, MEAT)

Pg 85

3	4	2	5	1
2	5	1	3	4
1	3	4	2	5
4	2	5	1	3
5	1	3	4	2

Pg 104 – 105

1. E
2. B
3. H
4. G
5. A
6. D
7. C
8. I
9. F

Pg 116 – 117

1. TRUE
2. TRUE
3. FALSE
4. TRUE
5. FALSE
6. TRUE
7. FALSE
8. TRUE
9. FALSE
10. FALSE
11. FALSE
12. TRUE
13. TRUE
14. FALSE
15. FALSE
16. FALSE
17. TRUE
18. FALSE
19. TRUE
20. FALSE

ACKNOWLEDGEMENTS

FRONT COVER © Shutterstock.com; (b) © Reuters/Cathal McNaughton, (tl) © Rex/Solent News;
BACK COVER (b) © www.flyingdog.us, (t) © Shutterstock.com;

4 (c/r) © Lonely - Shutterstock.com, Ivaylo Ivanov - Shutterstock.com, (t) © Dan Kosmayer - Shutterstock.com, (t/r) © RZ Design - Shutterstock.com, (c) © Alex Hubenov - Shutterstock.com, (b/r) © Rui Vieira/PA Wire/Press Association Images; **5** (b/l) © Kamonrat -Shutterstock.com, (c) © Rex/Solent News; **6—7** © Jeff Cremer; (b/l) © Eric Isselee - Shutterstock.com; **8** (t) © Lonely - Shutterstock.com, (l) © MSPhotographic - Shutterstock.com, (c) © Opas Chotiphantawanon - Shutterstock.com, (r) © Henrik Larsson - Shutterstock.com; **9** (l) © Nattilka - Shutterstock.com, (c) © FrameAngel - Shutterstock.com, (r) © Henrik Larsson - Shutterstock.com; **10—11** © nienora - Shutterstock.com; **12—13** © nienora - Shutterstock.com; **14** Rex/David Caird/Newspix; **15** (t) Rex/Andrew Tauber/Newspix, (b) Rex/David Caird/Newspix; **16—17** Rex/Brandon Goforth/Solent News; **18** (t) © Aaron Amat - Shutterstock.com, (c/l) © ajt - Shutterstock.com, (b) © Kotomiti Okuma - Shutterstock.com; **19** (t) © cellistka - Shutterstock.com, (b) © xavier gallego morell - Shutterstock.com **20** Imagine China; **21** Twin Design - Shutterstock.com; **22—23** Jeff Wright; **24** © Rex/Marc O'Sullivan, **25** © Martin Ellard/PA Archive/Press Association Images, **26** (t) Caters News, (b) Rex/Eye Ubiquitous; **27** (t) Allison Hoffman/Rex, (b) Rui Vieira/PA Wire/Press Association Images; **28** (t) © Bob Orsillo - Shutterstock.com; **29** Glenn Fuentes/AP/Press Association Images; **32** (t/l) © Aaron Amat - Shutterstock.com; **33** John Downer Productions/naturepl.com; **34** (t/r) Mitsuhiko Imamori/Minden Pictures/FLPA, (t/l) Carrie Vonderhaar/Ocean Futures Society/National Geographic Creative, (b) Thomas Marent/Minden Pictures/FLPA; **35** (t/r) Gerrit Vyn/naturepl.com; (b) Thomas Marent/Minden Pictures/FLPA; **36—37** Shutterstock.com; **38** (t) © Cultura/Photoshot, (b/l) Rex/Luka Esenko, (b/r) ThailandWildlife.com; **39** (t) Cassio Lopes/Caters News, (b/l) Michael Murphy, **40** (t) Fabio Pupin/FLPA, (b/r) Suzi Eszterhas/Minden Pictures/FLPA, (b/l) © Dr. Charles Mazel/Visuals Unlimited/Corbis; **41** (t/r) Choi Byung-kil/AP/Press Association Images, (l) Rex/Anne Ollila, (b/r) Alex Tyrrell/Caters News; **42** © Lonely - Shutterstock.com; **44** (t/l) Aarriene Van Schoonhoven/Mercury Press, (t/r) Jay Joslin/Mercury Press, (b) Tom Oliver/Mercury Press; **45** (t/l) David Dunsmore/Mercury Press, (t/r) Gini Reed/Mercury Press, (c/r) Tim Cordell/Mercury Press, (b) Steffen Kahl/Mercury Press; **46** Rex/M & Y News Ltd; **47** Rex/Mini; **48** (c/r, b/l) Shoe Bakery/ Rex; **49** (t/l) © Yaya Chou, (t/c) © Jeff Wright, (c/r) © Guzel Studio - Shutterstock.com, (c/l) © Mikey Jones/Caters News, (c) © Caters News, (c/r) © Rex/Eye Ubiquitous, (b/l) © www.flyingdog.us, (c/b) © Aaron Amat - Shutterstock.com, (b/r) © RZ Design - Shutterstock.com; **50** (t) © Guzel Studio - Shutterstock.com; **51** Nick Stoeberl; **52—53** Rex/Solent News; **54** © Javier Brosch - Shutterstock.com; **55** (t) © Alex Hubenov - Shutterstock.com, Eric Isselee - Shutterstock.com, Rex/Colin Hutton/Bournemouth News, Jennifer Sekerka - Shutterstock.com, © Norma Cornes - Shutterstock.com; **56** Rex/Mark Sisson, **57** (b/l) © Pan Xunbin - Shutterstock.com, (r) © maximult - Shutterstock.com; **60** © Rex/Andy Willsheer; **61** (b) © Dave Hersch/ Rex, (t) © Getty Images; **62** Reuters/Stringer; **63** (t) © Valentina_S - Shutterstock.com, (c/r) © MrGarry - Shutterstock.com, (b/r) © alexokokok - Shutterstock.com; **64** (t/l) Rex/M & Y News Ltd, (t/r) © David Carillet - Shutterstock.com, (b/l) Caters News; **65** (t) Rex/Lessy Sebastian/Solent News, (c) © Nattika - Shutterstock.com, (b/r) © javaman - Shutterstock.com; **66** © Rex/David Caird/Newspix; **67** (l) © Edward Westmacott - Shutterstock.com, (r) © Alex Hubenov - Shutterstock.com; **68** (l) © Smit - Shutterstock.com; **69** Rex/Jeremy Durkin; **70** (t) © smuay - Shutterstock.com, (b) © Melinda Fawver - Shutterstock.com; **71** © Alex Hubenov - Shutterstock.com; **72** (t) © Reuters/Cathal McNaughton, (c/r) © Reuters/Stringer, ajt - Shutterstock.com, (b) © Marcus Palmgren / BLT / SCANPIX/TT News Agency/Press Association Images, (b/r) © Kotomiti Okuma - Shutterstock.com; **73** Shutterstock.com; **74** (t) © Norma Cornes - Shutterstock.com, (b) © Javier Brosch - Shutterstock.com; **75** © szpeti - Shutterstock.com; **76** (t) © Lonely - Shutterstock.com, (l) © krichie - Shutterstock.com, anaken2012 - Shutterstock.com, (c) © Aaron Amat - Shutterstock.com, (r) © picturepartners - Shutterstock.com; **77** (l) © Dan Kosmayer - Shutterstock.com, (c) © Miguel Garcia Saavedra - Shutterstock.com, (r) © Africa Studio - Shutterstock.com; **80** © Suchatbky - Shutterstock.com; **81** © Eric Isselee - Shutterstock.com; **84** (r) © Henrik Larsson - Shutterstock.com, (l) © MSPhotographic - Shutterstock.com; **85** (b) © Henrik Larsson - Shutterstock.com, (l) © Nattilka - Shutterstock.com, (r) © FrameAngel - Shutterstock.com; **86—87** Rex/Colin Hutton/Bournemouth News; **88** (t/r) © Bildagentur Zoonar GmbH - Shutterstock.com, (c/l) © RedTC - Shutterstock.com, (c) © Sheli Jensen - Shutterstock.com, (c/r) © Aleksey Stemmer - Shutterstock.com, (b/l) © Eric Isselee - Shutterstock.com, (b/r) © NagyDodo - Shutterstock.com; **89** (t/l) Suren Manvelyan, (t/r) © Don Mammoser - Shutterstock.com, (c/r) © Robert Bagdi - Shutterstock.com, (b/l) © Liew Weng Keong - Shutterstock.com, (b/r) © Eric Isselee - Shutterstock.com; (r) Nick Garbutt/naturepl.com; **90** © Nathan Edwards/ Newspix/ Rex; **91** (t/l) © Jennifer Sekerka - Shutterstock.com, cellistka - Shutterstock.com, Kotomiti Okuma - Shutterstock.com, (r) © Alex Hubenov - Shutterstock.com, javaman - Shutterstock.com, (b) © Neil Lockhart - Shutterstock.com; **92** (t/r) You Touch Pix of EuToch - Shutterstock.com, (b) Marcus Palmgren/BLT/Scanpix/TT News Agency/Press Association Images; **93** © Eric Isselee - Shutterstock.com; **94—95** www.flyingdog.us; **98—99** Mauricio Handler/Handlerphoto.com/Solent; **100** © Rex/Solent News, (c/r, b/l) © Shoe Bakery/ Rex, (c/r) Shoe Bakery/ Rex; **101** (t/r) Mikey Jones / Caters News; **102** (t/r) © Africa Studio - Shutterstock.com; **103** (t, b/l) © Picsfive - Shutterstock.com, (c/l) © Tim UR - Shutterstock.com, (b/r) © Neil Lockhart - Shutterstock.com; **104** (t/r) © Africa Studio - Shutterstock.com; **105** © Africa Studio - Shutterstock.com, Picsfive - Shutterstock.com; **106** (c) Reuters/Sukree Sukplang, (b) Rex/Richard Austin; **107** (t) Rex/Media Mode Pty Ltd, (c) Reuters/Stringer, (b) Noah Goodrich/Caters News; **110** Thanh Ha Bui/HotSpot Media; **111** (b) Arsgera - Shutterstock.com; **112** (t/l) © Jennifer Sekerka - Shutterstock.com, (c/l) © Bahadir Yeniceri - Shutterstock.com, (c/r) © Ivaylo Ivanov - Shutterstock.com; **113** (b) © Eric Isselee - Shutterstock.com, (t/r) © gualtiero boffi - Shutterstock.com; **114** (t) © Borja Andreu - Shutterstock.com; **115** (c) © Volodymyr Krasyuk - Shutterstock.com, (b) © Ermolaev Alexander - Shutterstock.com; **116** (t) © Borja Andreu - Shutterstock.com; **117** (c) © Volodymyr Krasyuk - Shutterstock.com, (b) © Ermolaev Alexander - Shutterstock.com; **118** (t) © Lonely - Shutterstock.com, (l) © nito - Shutterstock.com, (c) © stockphoto-graf - Shutterstock.com, (r) © FrameAngel - Shutterstock.com; **119** (l) © Horiyan - Shutterstock.com, (c) © maxim ibragimov - Shutterstock.com, (r) © Africa Studio - Shutterstock.com; **120—121** AFP/Getty Images; **125** Dan Callister/Rex

Key: t = top, b = bottom, c = centre, l = left, r = right, sp = single page

All other photos are from Ripley Entertainment Inc. and Shutterstock.com.
Every attempt has been made to acknowledge correctly and contact copyright holders and we apologise in advance for any unintentional errors or omissions, which will be corrected in future editions.

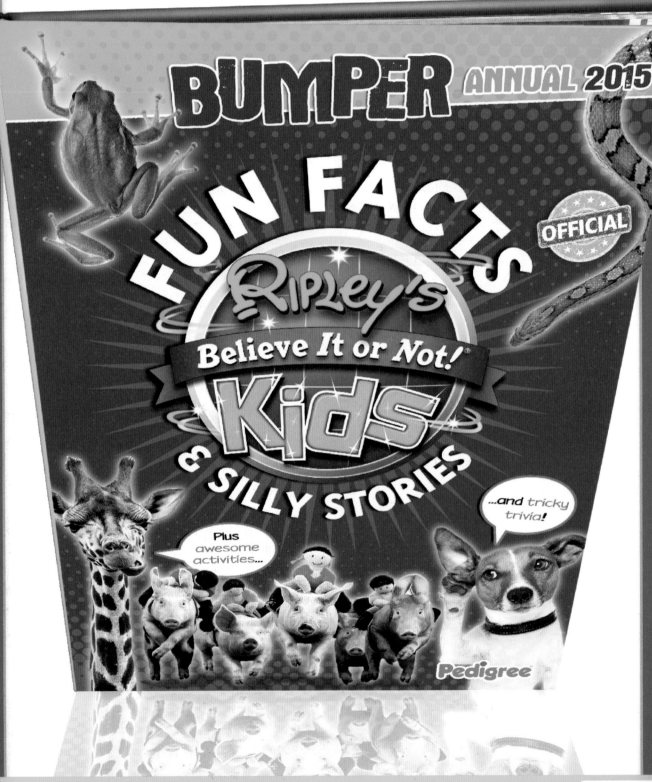